Being Human

you signed up for this

WELCOME

Sam Razberry

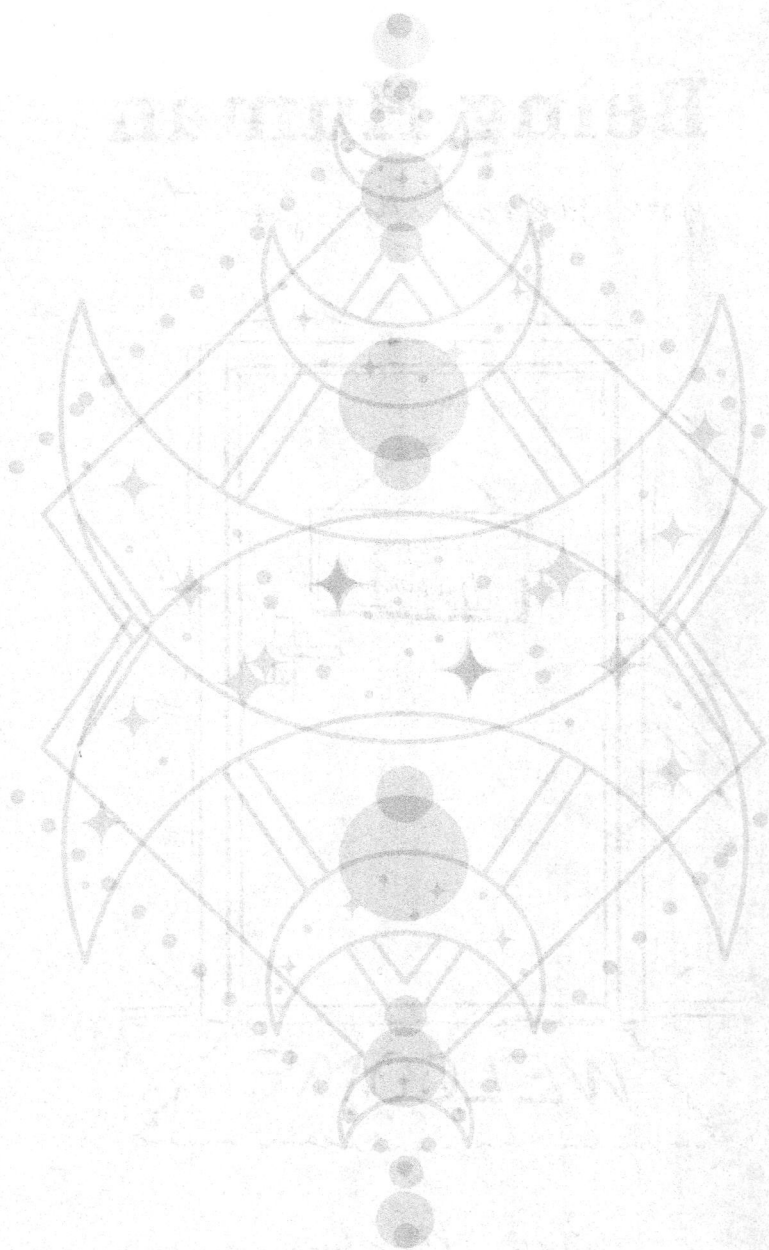

Being Human: You Signed Up For This
(2nd edition)
Copyright © 2022-2024 Sam Razberry
All Rights Reserved

ISBN: 979-8-9892133-2-0
eISBN: 979-8-9892133-3-7

Published by: Razberry Roots Publishing Co.
Cover design by: Sam Razberry

So, bless my heart
Bless my mind
I got so much to do
I ain't got much time
So, must be someone
Up above
Saying,
"Come on, girl, yeah.
You gotta get back up.
You got to hold on."

-Alabama Shakes

To my inner kid - who would like to thank: Winnie the Pooh, Bob Ross, Stuart the Pigacorn, Bigby Wolf & O'malley Cat, Stray Kids edits on YouTube, the lava lamp on my bedside, and all the love that surrounds me. Us.
Thank you. All of you.
(Especially Bigby, O'malley, & Stuart, obviously)

Contents

Your story

That's a wrap

Trigger Warning

It is with all the love I have to offer (which is a lot, by the way) that I ask you to enter this space with caution. Since its initial release in 2022, *Being Human* has been praised for its transparency and brutal honesty regarding the depth and intensity of feeling at any given moment. With that being said, I have also been told numerous times how my readers have had to step away, momentarily, when the content becomes darker than they expected. With that in mind, I decided to include a trigger warning in this edition.

The road ahead gets... rough, to say the least. Though there is light at the end of the tunnel, the journey there is dark. Please be advised, this book contains some pieces that center around or allude to SA, self-harm, and suicidal thoughts brought about by feelings of hopelessness and desperation. Please tread carefully as you move through the contents of both the poems in Part 1, and the invitation to journey inward in Part 2. In short, "Danger, Will Robinson, Danger".

Thank you. May the odds (and your fortitude) be ever in your favor.

Love always,

Raz

LOOK OUT
BIG FEELINGS AHEAD

Being Human Playlist

From as early as I can remember, music and expression through song have had my heart. The way a song can be heard at the same time by multiple people and mean something different to each one of them is much like reading poetry. What is a song if not poetry set to music? There are several songs on this playlist that could be interpreted in many ways. Some could be romantic or heart wrenching, dedicated to a lover or a friend. In the context of matching the vibes in *Being Human*, though, I wanted songs that could be from me to myself. Love letters and declarations of loss and longing that could be from my child self to my present, from me to my higher self, between my Self and the Universe.

Songs like *Fix You, Little Bird,* and *Self Help* feel like a conversation between my present self and the younger versions of me. I face releasing wounds around fear and lack in *ilomilo, Burning House,* and *New Person, Old Place.* In *Transatlanticism, Hellevator, Spirit Cold,* and *Mad World* I am crying out to the Universe, while it and my future self answer back in *Breathe Deeper, Hold On,* and *pretty when you cry.* Each song beautifully represents my journey back to my Self. I hope this playlist helps you dive deeper into your own experience with Being Human.

Track List

Being Human - Skrux, Mona Moua
Transatlanticism - Death Cab for Cutie
Spirit Cold - Tall Heights
Half Life - Duncan Sheik
Fix You - Coldplay
overwhelmed - Royal & the Serpent
Mad World - Michael Andrews, Gary Jules
Hellevator - Stray Kids
Hallucinogenics - Matt Maeson
You Found Me - The Fray
Burning House - Cam
Young Blood - Noah Kahan
ilomilo - Billie Eilish
Wishes - Tiny Habits
Cough Syrup - Young the Giant
Flight Risk - Tommy Lefroy
Anyway - Noah Kahan
City on a Hill - Mon Rovîa
Funny Story - Cate
Hold On - Alabama Shakes
Passenger - Noah Kahan
Step Into Your Power - Ray LaMontagne
You're Gonna Be Okay - Ashh Blackwood
It's Called: Freefall - Rainbow Kitten Surprise
Awaken - Stray Kids
Breathe Deeper - Tame Impala
Little Bird - The Weepies, Deb Talan, Steve Tannan
New Person, Old Place - Madi Diaz
Keep Breathing - Ingrid Michaelson

Big Love Ahead - Mon Rovîa
still feel. - half•alive
Older - Sasha Allen Sloan
Let Go - Frou Frou
Phobia - Stray Kids
Good Morning - Max Frost
Self Help - Olive Klug
Just Life - BLÜ EYES
Past Lives - BØRNS
Fly - Anna Graves
Mind on Fire - Aisha Badru
Jericho - Iniko
Celebrate - Tianda
pretty when you cry - Rachel Bochner
Holding Space - Mayyadda
I Think I'm Growing? - FLETCHER
I am YOU - Stray Kids
Actually Happy - BLÜ EYES
I Am Blessed - Desiree Dawson
New Bitch - Qveen Herby
Step Into My Power - Modern Headspace
When I Get There - Big Wild
You Signed Up For This - Maisie Peters

Scan the QR code &
click the spotify icon
to be taken directly
to *Being Human's*
playlist on Spotify.

Scan the QR code &
click the music icon
to be taken directly
to *Being Human's*
playlist on Apple
Music.

Part One
My Story

Being human

When I accepted
In the beginning
To come to this space
Of lessons and healing
I must have signed blindly
As I enlisted in life
Must have foregone the warnings
Guided only by light
They asked, and I answered
Seeking adventure, a quest
I was hardly concerned
Slightly cautious at best
Imagine my wonder
That growth would take payment
I must not have read
The fine print

So far so good?

Looking around it feels like
I must be doing this right
I am assimilating. Fitting in.
Mimicking the faces of those around me
This mask is... admittedly uncomfortable
Much like thin plastic facades
Worn on Halloween
This one digs in around my eyes
It makes it hard to breathe
I convince myself that
This is normal
This is good
I am good
Attempts to remove my mask prove...
Dangerous
Unappreciated
An accost to the sensitive sensibilities
Of family and friends
Somehow being ... myself?
Is offensive to those
Who only know how to be other
Who can I trust?
Not them, or them, or them
"Or you," I say
Pointing at myself in the mirror
Mask askew
Unnatural and off-putting
Dipping below my eyes
Revealing she who waits below the surface
Questioning and angry

Godless heathen

I pledge allegience
To your god
And yours
And yours
And yours
They're all the same
In different fonts
Each one
A different source
Of love
Of hate
And genocide
Of judgement evermore
Can't get it right
Don't follow light
For humans hold the score
I pledge allegiance
To the book
And its heresy within
I promise not to crumble
When life serves me a hand
That's scarred
And leaves me breathless
No footsteps in the sand
No guidance, only faith
Don't question where you stand
I pledge allegiance
To your god
The abandoner of man

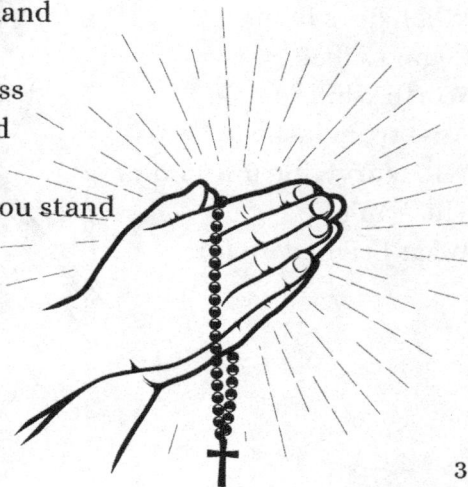

3

Something is missing

This vessel
Though mine from the start
Feels foreign
Floating above
I can see the void
It sits in my root
Steadily expanding
Creeping here and there
Until its presence is felt
All over
I can't escape this feeling
Trust me
I've tried
Through sabotage
And dissociation
I've attempted to flee
Everything I know
And everything I don't
This existence is
Exhausting
When does living
Begin to feel
Worth while?
Am I truly tasked
With surviving until I die?
This can't be
What I signed up for...

Secret secrets are no fun

From the quiet corners
In the back of my mind
Buried deep in my body
Came the voice of my youth
Timid, but resolute as she approached

"Can I... tell you a secret?
One nobody knows?"
I could feel her hesitation
What she carried
Was more than she could bear to hold

"Am I ready?
Will I survive knowing?"
She blinked
Something like frustration
Cast a shadow across her features

Her eyebrows rose, "I did."
There was an edge to her words
Like she was holding back rage
I couldn't blame her
She had kept me safe for long enough

"I'm sorry. You're right.
Thank you for carrying
What should have never
Burdened your young mind.
Thank you for waiting until I was ready."

She nodded, softening
"I don't wanna say it,
So I'm just gonna show you,"
She said, brandishing a chest
Rotting and thrumming from within

"Once you open this,"
She placed the putrid box in my hands
It was far heavier than I realized
"You won't ever be the same.
There's no going back to who you are now."

 I turned the vile thing over
Inspecting it from all sides
"Is there a trick to it?
Do I need to crack a code
Or solve some riddle for it to open?"

Her eyes locked on mine
I could feel her gaze burrow into my soul
"You need only be truly willing
To witness all your most hidden scars
Flayed open for you to tend to once and for all"

My eyes must have resembled saucers
Her phrasing caught me off guard
With words that sliced like a surgeon's knife
Ice cold and unfeeling
Aged beyond her small frame

She took my hand
Gently placing it atop the box
A rusted lock clicked
Popping the lid just enough
For darkness to ripple out like smoke tendrils

Our eyes met again
She was crying now
Or was that me?
Her little hand found mine
Squeezing my fingers in her fist

"You're so young. So small..."
My voice gave me away
Quavering and full of tears unshed
My throat bobbed
As realization dawned on me

"What... happened...
What happened to you?"
Her tiny fingers
The fingers of a two-year-old
Wrapped tighter around my own

"It's time to look in the box, now.
It's time to be brave."
We each glanced down at the chest
Taking in the last moments
Before knowing. Before everything changed.

"Will you be here with me?
While I face it?
Will you be here to hold my hand?"
She smiled now
"I'll always be here, all of us will be"

She gestured around
Revealing a four-year-old
Then seven, nine, thirteen
A sophomore, a senior
Then there were my twenties

I dropped to my knees
They were all carrying
Identical, decaying tombs
It became clear, by opening one
I'd be opening them all

She came to stand before me
Cupping my face in her hands
"This is not our end
We heal through your love
It is by your effort that we become *her*."

"Her?" I asked, confused
She beamed behind where I knelt
I turned to meet my own gaze
She was older and younger somehow
Filled with an exuberance that I had never known

"Oh," I was nearly speechless
She smiled tenderly at me
I could feel her appreciation
For the work I'd done thus far
And the work I'd do so she could exist

I was humbled into action
Courage and tenacity
Were all I had to go on
So I mustered both, and stood
Readying myself for the journey ahead

"You signed up for this, you know"
Whispered my future with a coy grin
"You're more than ready.
You were built for this, and you *will* succeed."
Her faith stirred my own

Surrounded by all of me
I peered down at the waiting chest
Wanting, begging to open
As if carrying its secrets
Was as much a burden for it, as it was for me

"I am willing and able to embark on this journey.
Show me what I've kept hidden from myself."
The chest flew open, all light was gone
Darkness entombed us as I took my first step
Traversing the void with only my selves to guide me

His name is burned in my memory

I shouted at myself
"Show me, show me now!"
As I held open my tender lids
His face came into view
My mind's eye flooded
With the color of his hair
The scent of his breath
The grip of his fist
Nausea permeated through my being
I usually remember
From outside of myself
Yet, this time
For this memory
I was in my body
Too young...
I was too young
I didn't fight him
I didn't know I should
A body so innocent
Defiled by the hand
Of a trusted adult
My nerve endings died that day
Leaving me numb
To the touch of another
I'll see his face
Every
Single
Day
Until I find a way
To mend the girl
He left behind

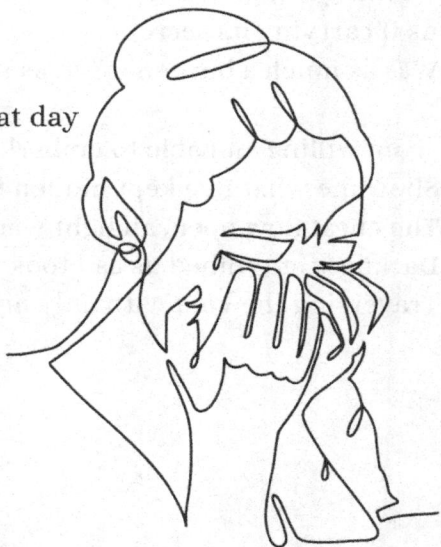

So begins the task of unearthing myself

I am
But an exposed
Raw
Festering
Wound
Bleeding all over
Myself and my loves
A burden to care for
A burden to Be
At least...
That's what my mind
Tortured and defeated
Convinces me to believe
I pick myself apart
Bit by crumbled bit
Sifting through the rubble
That is my mind, body
And soul
Searching for anything
Everything
That resembles
Even a semblance
Of myself
Whoever
That
Is

Metamorphosis or bust

What has been unleashed
Clangs around in my body
Like a pinball searching for secrets
Through portals and trap doors
It demands I leave behind
What no longer serves
Including pieces of myself
A career of healing touch
Results in the abandonment
Of client and friend
I can no longer touch
The skin of another
When my own feels
Raw and inflamed
A dream of motherhood
Rips from my being
An organ meant for creating life
Steals from my own
While refusing to render children
Connections with others
Thought to be evergreen
Fall away like leaves in Autumn
A vessel crumbles from within
Crying out from its self-destruction
Desperate to purge, to fall apart
I hold a funeral for my ego death
A melted carcass inside my cocoon
Destroying myself for the sake of myself
All in the name of a breath worth taking

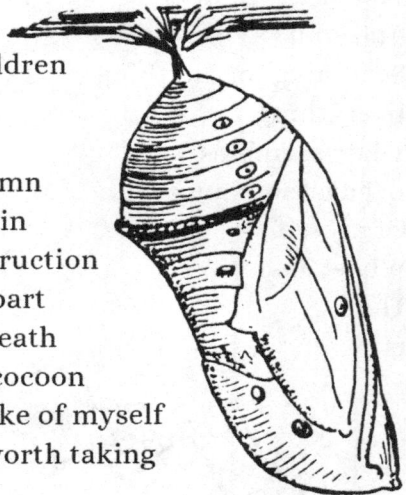

Wombless

There's a scar
On my belly
Below my navel
Where you'll never exist
Light pink from time passing
Where the physical body has healed
But the emotional body has not
A reminder of a decision
One made for me
A choice I never chose
A timestamp
When my world stopped
And spun backwards on its axis
There's a scar
My finger traces
Each time I remember
Where you'll never exist

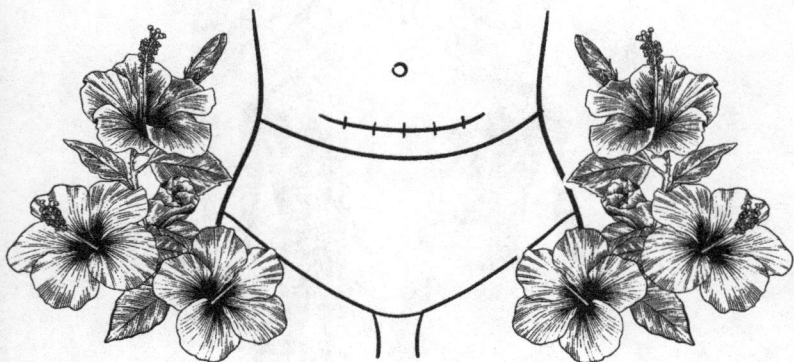

I'm coming undone

I'm feeling undone

my undoing
leaves me feeling
undone

My Undoing
Leaves Me Feeling
Undone

MY UNDOING
LEAVES ME FEELING
UNDONE

I'm feeling undone

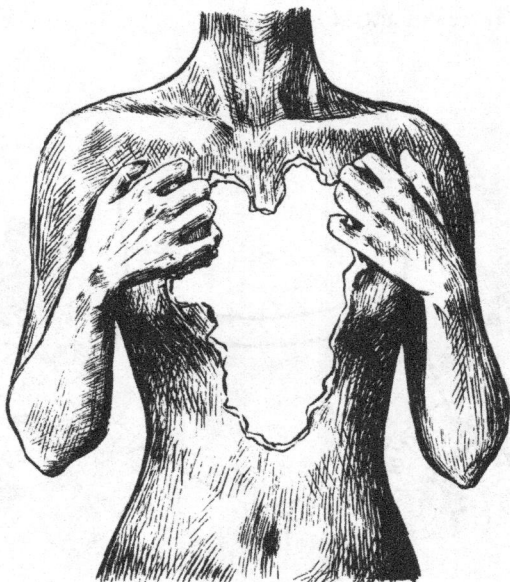

Overwhelmed

My heart is steady racing
Too many beats to count
Catch me crying on the floor
Feels like I'm dying now
Lift me up, your hand in mine
Help me breathe again
Turn on the light, please be my guide
Remind me who I am
See me through me
Because I can't
Hold the mirror up
Coach me, "Inhale. Exhale," now
I need to fill my cup
Bring me back here to myself
Assure me pain's receding
Until I feel my soul again
My reflection does the leading

What can I do?

I hate I cannot save you
He said with heavy heart
I want to put you back to rights
But don't know where to start
There are no maps or tools
No signs with arrows guiding
I want to slay your demons now
But don't know where they're hiding
I can only hold you close
Convince you of your brilliance
I'll stand guard, await the day
I witness your resilience

Ideations

A fork in a socket
A turn of the wheel
A bath with a toaster
Just so I don't feel
A few pills too many
The slice of a knife
Is all it would take
To exit this life
Call me a coward
For wanting to leave
Drown me in judgement
Until I can't breathe
Tell me I'm selfish
That I don't know strife
You only add reasons
To exit this life

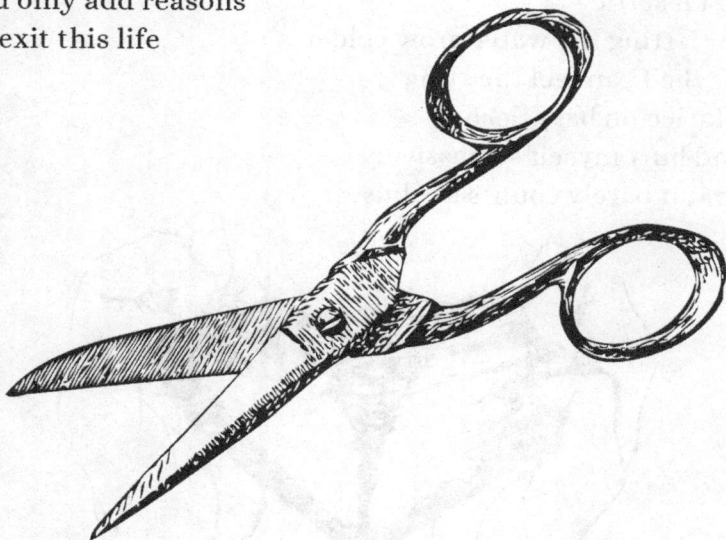

Cutting isn't my style

How nice it would be
For this tepid shower
To grow scalding
Set my skin aflame
Singe the surface
Singe the soul
I made my home
On the floor of the tub
I had been crying
For longer than I realized
Begging, aching
For release from this suit
Taxing the hot water supply
Beyond its means
So I'll settle
For letting the water grow colder
Maybe I can feel the sting
Like ice on bare flesh
And hurt myself so passively
That it barely counts as abuse

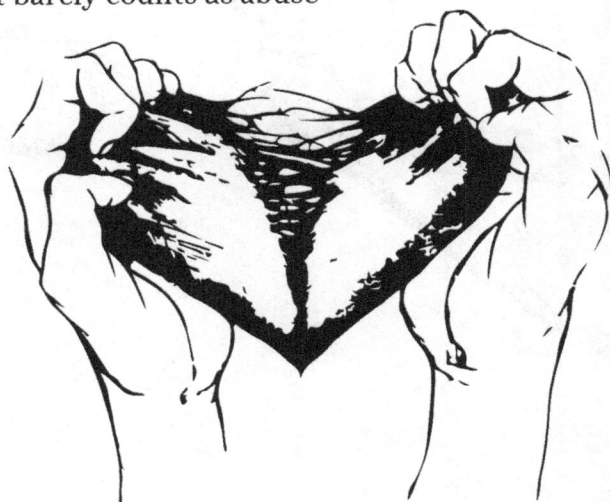

Soothing self-harm

The brain is a bully in a quiet room
If you lack the proper restraints
It will run reckless and with purpose
Knocking over precious heirlooms
Sullying perfectly fine memories
Intrusive and entitled in nature
Attempts to hush its string of insults fall short
Pleading offers only momentary relief
As it requires catharsis to cease its rampage
I ball my fists
And sink my nails into flesh
Just hard enough to sting
Distracting the beast
From its path of destruction
Long enough to salvage what remains
Crescent moons paint a bizarre sky
Across both my palms
Revealing secrets
I am never ready to tell

It's the duality for me

How am I
The light
That shines for others
A brilliant glow in the dark
As well as
The flickering bulb
Of an old lamp
Whose cord is frayed
Dangerous at best
When it comes to
Illumination for myself
How can I be both?

All that I know is I'm breathing

As I sink into my body
I can feel her presence again
My youth joins me on the floor
And quietly wraps her arm around me
She has grown since we last spoke
Her energy, like my own, is both
Heavy and light
Wearying and enlivening
Uplifting and arduous all at once
The juxtaposition of it all
Wreaks havoc no matter the balance
Until I am left toilworn
In the midst of unbridled chaos
Ever seeking the eye
Any port in the storm
To center and ground
We stay there silently together
Everything we need to say
Sent through our fingertips
Like signals relayed
Through trees' tangled roots
"I see you"
"I love you"
"I'm here"
"We can do this"
On and on
For days and weeks
And months on end
Breathing life into the other
Until we are born anew

A taste of transcendence

Dive deep in this crevice of immortality
Hoping to find some clue to life
Knowing that somewhere there's hidden reality
Breathing the essence of craving the light

Creating a tomb for my soul's aggravation
While mending the heart that's been slain
Battling thoughts of total extinction
Suspicious of rivals inflicting the pain

Wary of wolves who've destroyed me once
Of the thorns in the bushes of scorn
Leaning on those who don't join in the hunt
But who offer a flower to mourn

Retreat into caves to protect my soft skin
To learn how to feel without fear
Leading with love I will step out again
With courage and grace I appear

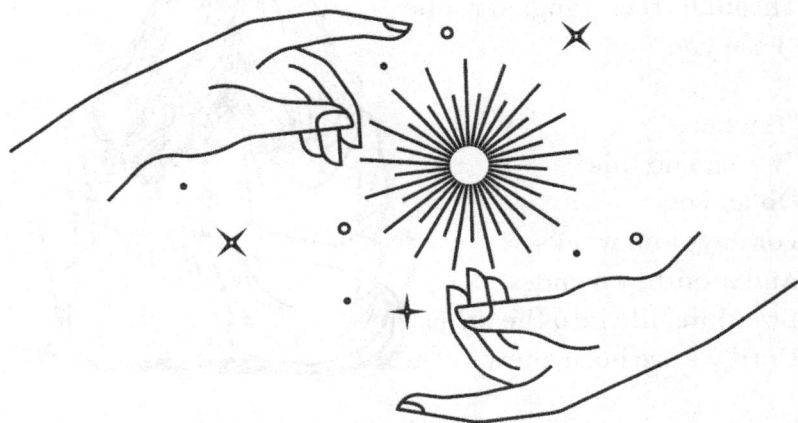

Conversations with the Universe

Am I doing this right?

How do you mean?

Am I *doing* this right?

What are you saying?

Am I growing and shedding
Learning, not dreading
Am I living the way
You would want me to live?

Do you need my approval?
Does it cause upheaval?
Do you fear I would shame
The dire straits that you're in?

Hmm...
I guess it sounds silly

I only wish really
To witness you thrive
And not just survive
But that comes with learning
Stop wishing and yearning
For growth doesn't flow
When you're fighting

Oh, baby baby

Babies, Babies everywhere
But none inside of me
Baby's, Baby's tears are shed
But this time Baby's me

Babies, Babies in my care
But never in my womb
Baby's, Baby's got a scar
Revealing Baby's tomb

Babies, Babies not my own
But that's not how it feels
Baby's, Baby's heart's undone
But that's how Baby heals

Over the river & through the woods

The night drags on
Ever lengthening as it goes
Until there is nothing left to do
But flourish in the dark
I take my cues from midnight bloomers
And creatures who thrive
When the sun descends below the horizon
I am led by fire flies
To groves of moonflowers
Glowing as they blossom
For the moon and stars alone
Bats, owls, and luna moths
Guide me ever onward
Each step I take
Leads me further through the gloom
My nocturnal companions
Bestow me with gifts
Superior vision and flight
Enlightening my path and mind
So that I may soar through the darkness
With ample trust and confidence
In my ability to withstand the unknown
They call to me
Compelling and earnest
Chirping, screeching, cooing
"The only way out is through"

Surrender to the process

Floating
Then
Flailing
Then
Drowning
Then
Wailing
Then
Grasping
Then
Prevailing
Then
Floating
Then...

This heart is a haunted house

They say what you don't know
Won't hurt you
What you don't explore
Won't haunt you
I call bullshit
Even the ghosts you can't see
Will manifest in the sounds
Of quiet cries
Footsteps at your door
Fear in your heart
I choose to adventure instead
Ask the ghosts to show themselves
Give them space to be
Then kindly and gently
Send them on their way
Exorcizing the spaces left to rot
Baptizing myself in grace

It's a syndrome

"imposter
Imposter
IMPOSTER!"
My fears would shout
Drowning out any imaginary credibility
I would attempt to establish for my brain
Whose fragility is illustrated
By its inability to quiet these intrusions
The moment they arise
"I am not the imposter,"
I say to myself
"It is *you*, Fear, that lies
And creates false narratives for me to ingest
Unquestioningly and doe-eyed.
It is *you* that poisons my mind
Who is wanting and ready
To believe every toxic word you would whisper
In hopes of bringing about my demise."
I close my eyes and remind myself I belong
The true imposter retreats for another day
Into the dark where it feeds on inhibitions
And scarcity mindset to survive
Slowly but surely
I starve it
To death

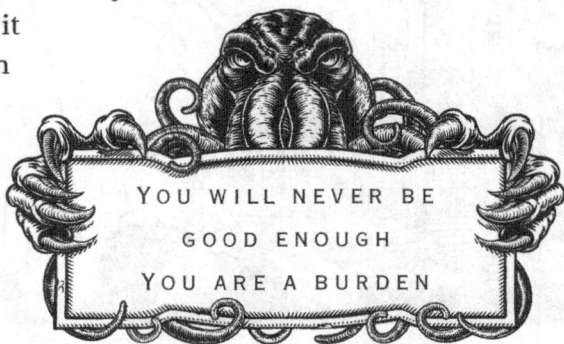

YOU WILL NEVER BE
GOOD ENOUGH
YOU ARE A BURDEN

You better work

Processing looks like
A bathtub filled
Again and again
It smells like
Earth Mother's
Medicine
Deep breaths
Tears flowing
It sounds like
A melody meant
For diving deeper
For creating harmony
From dissonance
Processing feels like
Ripping off the bandage
For opening wider
The wound that ails me
Allowing emotions
To flow freely
Like hemorrhaging
For the benefit
Of my Being
With trust
And faith
I won't
Bleed
Out

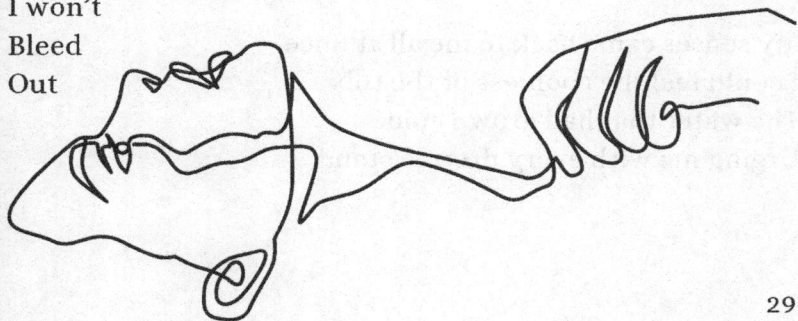

She came from the dark

Collapsed, weeping
And barely able to breathe
Craving release from this life
Unable to lift my voice to cry for help

My eyes searched for a way out
That's when I saw it
The sharp-edged key
That unlocked my exit

My shadow slinked to my side
"You're all alone, now
Not a *soul* is coming
To save you"

For a terrifying moment
I believed her
Reaching for my escape
I caught a glimpse of myself

From outside of my body
I watched as I entertained
The overwhelming urge to end it all
It was enough to remind me who I am

My senses came back to me all at once
I could feel the coolness of the tub
The water that had grown cold
Urging me with every drop to stand

Strength that was buried
Picked me up from my knees
My legs, shaking, held strong
I said to her, but mostly myself

"I am not alone
I have *me*
I save me
I am enough"

She smirked and slithered away
Primed for the next opportunity
To start fires
In a drought

Cheers to our timely demise

"You just have
So much going on"
You said through text
Cowardly and effortless
I could have expected as much

"It's a lot, Sam
I can't be the person
You lean on for support"
I'd known that, yet I had resisted
Parting seemed impossible before then

"I'll always care for you
I will always be your friend"
Liar. You're lying. You always lie
You were making it easy to let you go
I guess I should appreciate you for that

Day after passing day
It became abundantly clear
How stunted I was from the years
Spent holding your hand, pulling you on
All in a trauma driven attempt to keep you close

I can now confidently say
I am grateful we parted ways
I hope your life is filled with love
You would only accept the bare minimum
I hope someday you find yourself worthy of more

And so it went
Friends and family
Turned former and foe
When my growth became
Too much. Too often. Too heavy

One by one
They fall away
Fleeing from the mirror
Until only the steadfast remain
We happily evolve in tandem, side by side

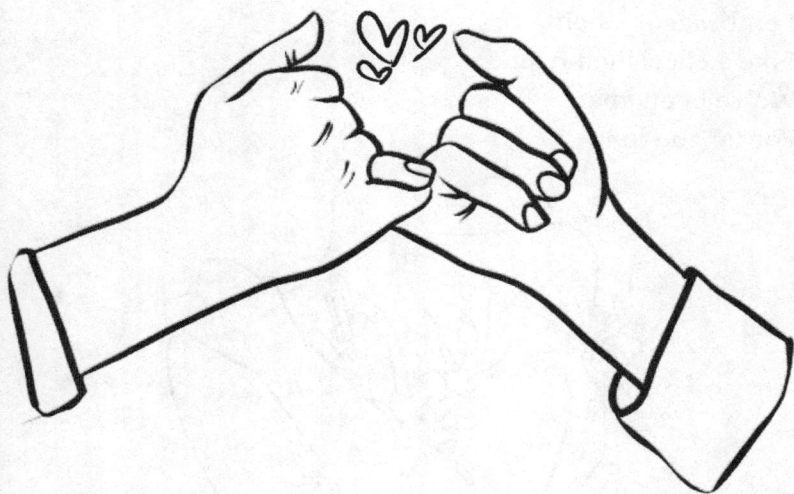

Reunited

I stretch into my skin
From my crown
To the tips of my toes
Allow myself to feel
Each and every part of me
The soft curves
The jagged edges
The pieces that feel foreign
I fill my body with my Self
And remember who I am
Has it really been ages
Since I've felt alive?
I embrace my being
Like a cherished friend
We've been apart
For far too long

Fresh air, fresh perspective

My breath flows with ease
Effortless as rivers winding
Crisp like autumn leaves
No need for coaching
It's not fall or winter
Yet here I am
Feeling rejuvenated
By the very air
That grew toxic
When I thought
Life was only pain
I pull it into my chest
In big gulps like cold water
To wash away the faraway notion
That one more breath
Could kill me

Coming home

There is a place
Where water meets the earth
Surrounded by hills and grace
Where the depths of my breath
My love and my life
Rival the miles of lake around me
Whose siren song
Whispered through trees and daydreams
Has reached my ears
And enveloped my heart in hope
There swims the promise
Of peace and love
Everlasting
My fears are swept away
I am safe
The current rushes
To welcome me home

To acknowledge is to heal

They'll say, "The past is in the past,"
And on this we agree
But the wounds inflicted in my past
Travel with me presently

Not lightened scars from healing
With love and tender care
But gaping masses crudely patched
By a brain too young to bear

"The past is in the past,"
So is my child mind
Warped and rotting from within
From the secrets that it hides

You can find me tending
To my scars with gentle grace
Applying salves and ointments
Allowing healing to take place

Those marring wounds that fester
May their presence never last
So that I may truly say
"The past is in the past"

THE STAR

I will cut you with love and boundaries

I am soft
Like a feather-down pillow
A comfortable place to land
To soothe away
A trying day

I am sharp
Like a knife poised and ready
To slice the ties that bind
Creating space
Where once was none

I am love
Presented in all forms
Fluctuating to and fro
To serve me
To save me

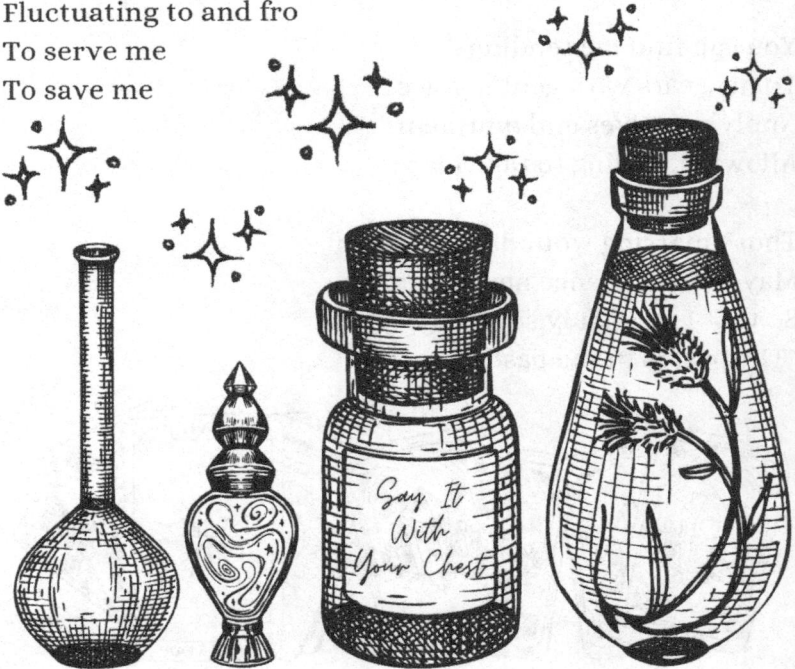

Say It
With
Your Chest

Integrating

I am neither
Good nor bad
I simply Am

I am neither
Broken nor healed
I simply Am

I am neither
Light nor shadow
I simply Am

Growing
Brave
Loved beyond measure
I simply Am

May they be ever in your favor

What incredible opportunities

We're offered in this life

The odds we face to learn and grow

To survive is biological

To *live* is a choice

To love against every odd

To experience gratitude against every odd

To simply exist and *be* against every odd

They could be stacked against you

Or feel like friends by your side

Oh, the odds this life can provide

Moonlight Rituals

The moon ever glowing
Bathes me in light
And envelops my being in grace
I am baptized in her waves
And left gently renewed
Our ritual cleanses my soul
She greets me each evening
A comforting constant
A beacon in the midst of uncertainty
Our natural rhythms synchronize
As we dance through our phases in tandem
She never baulks at my fullness
I never judge her shadow
We simply witnesses the other
With admiration and awe
Ever growing as we cycle
Refuel, release, realign
Again and again
Relishing the night
Together

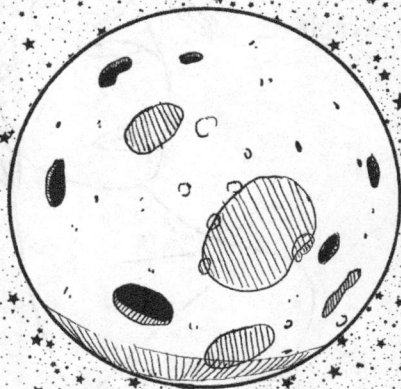

Unwavering

I love myself
On a bright, warm day
When the sun kisses my skin

I love myself
When others
Accept me as I am

I love myself
On a dark, lonely night
When all reason and light feels lost

I love myself
When others reject me
When I feel unseen and alone

Against all odds
All the time
At every turn
I love myself

It's the little things

It's the way I strive to give
As much as I receive
The way I see pain as a stepping stone
An opportunity for growth
It's the tea label I use as a bookmark
My hoard of coloring books
And magical stones
Scattered 'round the house
It's my sense of wonder
And my awe of the sunset
It's my care for others
And an ever expanding heart
Despite the risks that come
With unbridled love
It's every bit of me
That makes me cherish
Who I am

Loved by me

Looking back on you
And all that you've been through
I'm seeing you, I'm holding you
Please know you're loved by me

Looking back on you
And all you'll have to lose
I'm seeing you, I'm holding you
Please know you're loved by me

You are enough
You *are* enough
Please know you're loved by me

Your heart is tender
Your skin is tough
Please know you're loved by me

Continue on
Resolve is strong
Please know you're loved by me

Ego death
Release what's left
You know you're loved by me

Self-love

"You're back"
I said with a smile
My youth skipped
Nearly weightless
To join me by the sea
We stood arm in arm
Admiring the waves
Cerulean like the sky above them
"The storm is gone"
She spoke with an audible grin
And something else...
"Are you... proud of me?"
Our world brightened
At the glow in her cheeks
As she leaned into me, giggling
"More than you know. We all are.
You've brought us to life
Back from a fate worse than death
Rescued us from hiding
Pulled us from the
Rot and rubble
How could we love you more?"
I laughed now
"I'm sure you'll find a way"
She nodded, knowingly
And turned back to the sea
Raising a hand to the sky
Signaling peace and love
Everlasting

You signed up for this

So, here I am - despite myself
And my frequent wishes to the contrary
I reside here against my will
Yet still somehow in accordance with it
A burning desire to be both
Raging fire and rushing water
Blinding light
And the very essence of the dark itself
Seeking an abundance of peace
Only ever resulting from great unrest
I frequently remind myself
When the waters turn to rapids
And the fire singes my skin
That I came here voluntarily
Of my own volition
Signed my name on the dotted line
And after all this
The heartache
The laughter
The utter loneliness at times...
If I had the chance
To do it over again
I still wouldn't read
The fine print

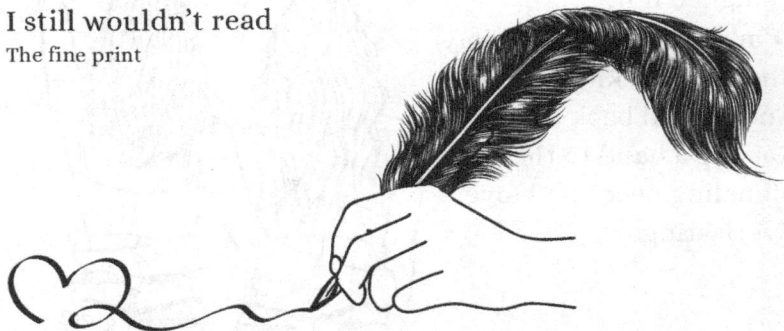

Part Two
Your Story

An Adventure in Self-Discovery

Feeling disconnected from your inner child? Maybe you're in the mood for a little shadow work? Or perhaps you're here to delve into the depths of your heart to see what you find. No matter your motivation, these prompts are sure to get you exploring your inner world. Remember to be gentle, compassionate, and kind with yourself as you venture inward to uncover your own wounds and opportunities for growth and healing. Stop when you need a break- the journey is always here for you to pick back up when you are ready. Good luck, you brave explorer, you.

It's Dangerous to Go Alone, Take This

An adventurer is only as formidable as the tools at their disposal. In 2019, at the beginning of this journey to discovering my Self, I was nearly torn apart by what I uncovered. Flashbacks plagued nearly every moment of every day- and night- to the point of wanting to end it all. I wasn't sure if I would ever feel better; if I'd ever go a day without seeing the face of those who had hurt me in the front of my mind. If not for the tactics I learned along the way, I might not be here. It was through developing a care tool kit that I was able to not only survive, but eventually thrive. Had I known then what I know now, I would have loaded my supply bag from the start with all that I have learned. Since I can only do so much work for my past self, I felt it was important to encourage *you* to set yourself up for success before ever beginning your inner work. Learning how best to regulate your nervous system during a flare, knowing who you can lean on for support, and integrating self-care practices into your day will help tremendously in not only being a person in general, but with the daunting- albeit rewarding- task of traversing your inner world.

Choose Your Weapon

Here are a few of the regulation methods and resources I use when I am facing down a flare, plus a few more. Please take some time to research these methods, and experiment to find what works best for you:

- 4 x 4 breathing (box breathing)
- somatic movement
- vagus nerve stimulation
- eft tapping
- gentle tapotement across the chest and back of legs (percussive cupping/tapping/slapping)
- therapy (talk, neurofeedback, emdr, art, etc)
- phone a friend (even better, have a codeword you can text when you're in need of grounding)
- grounding exercises (literally touch grass/hug trees, yin yoga, 5 4 3 2 1 grounding method)
- *SAFE* cathartic activities (scream into a pillow, shoot some baddies in a video game, tear up old clothing/sheets/towels, rage room)
- The Busyhead Project: Founded by Noah Kahan, The Busyhead Project works to destigmatize mental health and provide resources for individuals in need of care, as well as for those that love someone with a Busyhead. Find more information and a invitation to donate at busyheadproject.org.
- Project Healthy Minds: PHM is a mental health initiative that strives to make finding the mental health support for you as easy as possible with the world's first mental health marketplace. They work to demonstrate the need for mental health support in the workplace, and also offer free, 24/7 crisis support. Text HOME to 741741 or visit projecthealthyminds.com for a safe space to land.

Visualization Work

This will vary depending on the circumstances and situations you are facing, and will likely differ from person to person. In the journaling section ahead, I walk you through a visualization that I use myself. In my own work, I tend to hold these younger versions of myself, & affirm their feelings. "I am sorry this happened to you. I am here, now, and you are safe. Your fear/anger/sadness is valid, but no longer serve our journey. Let's release this together." This isn't a cure-all, and the way you show up for yourself each time you do this practice will shift according to the emotions coming up. Sometimes, I would "simply" pull myself out of a dangerous environment, and repeat loving affirmations to that version of myself. Other times, I imagined unleashing my rage upon those that harmed me, tearing them to shreds over and over until the fire dissipated. How you are feeling at any given moment will oftentimes determine how your inner child wants you to release. Remember, anger and sadness are not "bad" emotions. They are simply showing you where your pain is present, and where your needs are unmet. They come up to serve a purpose, to be acknowledged, honored, and released.

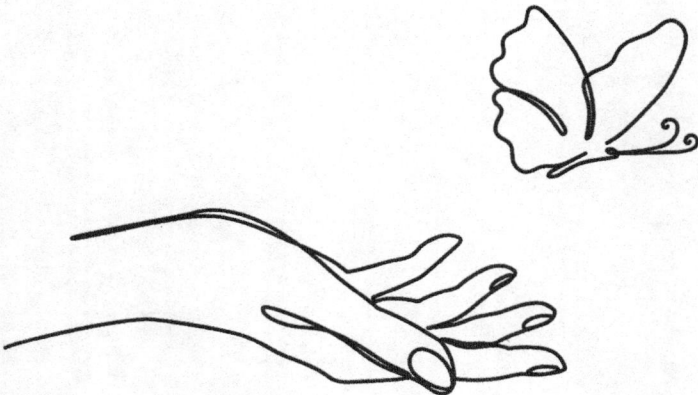

Build Your Arsenal

Before you move forward, take this opportunity to list out your support staff. Whether that looks like support friends, music, joy building activities, somatic exercises, self care routines (or all of the above and more), listing out all the ways you help yourself weather the storm is a tool in and of itself. Often, in times of high stress we struggle to remember everything we have in our toolbox. This list will help you remember the methods you know have worked for you. Add to it as you discover more ways to support your journey.

Soundtrack Your Life

What songs soundtrack your life? From heartache to elation, what tunes would you pick to showcase your journey here, Being Human? Craft your own life's vibe in a playlist, then give it a listen. How does it flow? What feelings does it bring up? Here's to your melodious heart mending adventure.

"It's time to look
in the box, now.
It's time to be **brave**."
We each glanced down
at the chest
Taking in the last moments
Before knowing.
Before everything changed.

Let's start with a visualization exercise. Close your eyes and imagine you're standing outside the door to your heart. You've come here to connect with your inner child. What does the door look like? Is it standing alone, or is it attached to a structure? Take a moment to describe what you see.

_____

_____

_____

_____

_____

_____

_____

_____

Now, imagine knocking, and gently asking that the version of you who needs love to come to the door. Who shows up? How old are they? What time frame in your life did they come from? What emotion comes with them?

_____

_____

_____

_____

_____

_____

_____

_____

_____

_____

_____

_____

_____

_____

_____

_____

_____

_____

If you feel safe and ready, ask that they share insights behind triggers, fears, or phobias that you struggle with. What holds you back from thriving? What childhood moments shaped the way you respond to stressors? Take some time to explore and describe what you discover.

Imagine accompanying them back to the timeframe they came from. If you find them in a traumatic space, take this opportunity to pull them from the situation, and provide them with the love and protection you needed at the time. Describe how you were called to support them in the moment they brought you to (see "It's Dangerous to Go Alone" for examples of how this might look).

This is the method I personally use when intentionally turning inward to gently dig into the hurt parts of myself. Oftentimes, I will follow up with a grounding session (usually a salt bath to replenish nutrient levels that can be affected by emotional upheaval) while I listen to hertz music geared toward energetic and emotional healing. I also like to journal anything else that comes up as a result of the work I did. Take these next pages as an opportunity to journal, scribble, doodle, or otherwise process your adventure inside yourself.

Works by this Author

Published:
From Soil to Sun and Back Again

Our author is a fan of two things in life: condiments, and a really great (though painstakingly thought out at times), ~~longwinded~~ metaphor. Armed with restaurant ranch dressing ("Could I get extra sauce?") and a smooth-writing clicky pen, she continued her journey to the core of her Being through writing poetry disguised as (you guessed it) metaphors for plant growth.

We all have our growing seasons, sure, but what about the time spent nestled away from the world pursuing our most evolved selves? What of the growing pains, the root rot, the too-small pots? Read along through all her life cycles (so far). From a sapling, back to a seed, to bloom, to wither, to revive herself, and grow From Soil to Sun & Back Again.

Razberry Writes & Rambles (podcast)

"Hellooo, Light Lovers" I am a published poet, retired massage therapist, lifetime writer and creator, and official dispenser of care bear stares. It is my intention to expand my understanding of myself and the universe, as well as inspire others to do the same. Join me on my journey as I share my work and many musings on self-reflection, embrace my shadow work, and dish on all my most anxiety ridden moments where I came out on the other side alive and well...ish. "You know what time it is... I Love You. Until next time, Peace, Love, and Taco Grease."

Coming Soon:
Forget My Name (Father's Day 2025)

This novella centers on Jenna Anne- Annie to her dad, Luke...until now. Upon hearing her estranged father has developed dementia and has subsequently erased her from his mind, she is given a choice. She can walk away forever- he doesn't even know she exists, after all- or she could harness this opportunity to interact with him like never before: as a stranger that receives the best of him, just like strangers always have. The best he never gave to her. Will remaining anonymous prove safe enough to take what she can get? Or will her quest to be known as herself task her with more to traverse than she expected?

Speaking of Love (2026)

Love isn't always romantic. There's platonic love. Familial love. Self love. I'll be exploring the depth, elation, & heartache that comes with all the different kinds of loving in this continuation of my poetry chapbook series. It will also come with its own soundtrack on Spotify to listen along while reading for an immersive experience sure to get you in your feels.

Project: "Hiraeth" (2027)

This yet-to-be-named book will center around our protagonist, Margo- a wily red-headed girl who is anything but average. Follow along as she discovers her life isn't all she thought it was, and why she's always felt so alone in her own company. Could there be a soul mate out there to fill the void of companionship? Will she accept the quest to find herself left behind by her now missing Gram? You'll have to travel the seas and stars to find out.

Sneak Peak: Forget My Name

prologue
happy birthday to you

Every year around my birthday, when the nights grow longer and daylight is in short supply, my father loses his grip on reality, abandoning rational thought, and runs away with delusion. This year, though, he had been steady, present. I had let down my walls and tiptoed into trust... Just in time for him to flip the script.

My phone buzzed, lighting up to reveal "Daddio" was calling a few days after my birthday. I joyfully picked up, prepared for one of our signature banter sessions with silly voices and laughing so hard my stomach hurt.

"Oh helloooo!" I said in my worst British accent.

His greeting was less than warm, and leaned heavily into a version of him I hadn't seen in at least a year and a half. So began the onslaught of religious harassment I had heard so many times before.

"I don't understand. Where is this coming from? I... I..." I stammered, then stopped to gather myself.

"I thought you were calling to wish me a happy birthday," I said in a near-whisper. I could feel my heart breaking in that old familiar way. It somehow stung more than ever. I had really let myself believe we had made progress in his understanding of my stances on faith, spirituality, karma, and being a good human for the sake of being kind and loving and gentle. Brave for the sake of being soft. Loving recklessly for the lessons of it all. Becoming more and more myself by the day, and spreading light all the way. He was curious, non-judgmental. It was a wild improvement to being berated for not aligning with his exact brand of connectedness. At the end of the day, we both felt connected to a higher energy, agreeing we simply called it by different names.

This call felt as if that moment had never occurred. It made me question my sanity... *Did that happen?*

He doubled down, spewing the ill-contrived gospel of a man undone. I flew from sadness to anger.

"This is the last time I'm going to tell you this, Luke. My relationship with God is my own. Please stop shoving your dogma down my throat." I could hear him flinch at the sound of his name leaving me with such animosity.

"Dad. I am your **dad**, as much as you **hate** that."

"I don't hate that you are my father. I hate that you can't seem to respect me or anything I have to say for the sheer fact that I am your daughter. Why can't you just let me be? Why can't you just be happy that I am a good person, that I treat others with kindness?" I muttered to myself, "Often kinder than what others deserve."

"I heard that," he spat.

"Good, I'm glad to see your selective hearing is operating at peak performance."

We sat in silence until he let out a loud, dramatic, breath.

"Baby, I know you think your old man is just talking out of his ass, but I am divinely blessed. I have a direct connection to God Almighty, and I know if you don't give your heart to Jesus, you will face an eternity in Hell. I just don't want that for you. I'm trying to save you, just like I strive to save others. There will come a day when someone will recognize you on the street- they'll know you're my daughter- and they will shake your hand and tell you with tears in their eyes that your dad helped lead them to Jesus Christ. I am a profit of the Lord. You can believe whatever you want, but- unless you align yourself with God- you are walking a path of damnation."

I felt my consciousness snap in jagged halves. How could we be having this conversation again. How- after the longest stint we've had of peace and a semblance of mutual acceptance and understanding- were we here **again**. How could I have let myself become so comfortable with our rapport that I forgot who he has always been?

"You told me you understood what my spirituality looks like. You told me it sounds like your connection with God. You told me! YOU TOLD ME YOU ACCEPTED ME THE WAY THAT I AM!!"

"Annie, please, you know I can't remember everything. Not since the wreck. There are so many holes in my memory. So many stories of yours I have no recollection of. All I know for certain is no amount of 'spiritual connection'," his air quotes were audible, "is a replacement for giving your life over to God."

I was fuming. My heartbeat sounded in my ears like war drums on distant battlefields. My hands shook as I held myself back from launching my phone into the fresh coat of dreamy blue paint on my bedroom wall. I had answered his call in the midst of happily painting, dancing, and singing as I worked to enhance my space.

"That's it. I'm done." I said with such stillness it made even *me* shudder.

"Done with what?" His voice sounded far away, as if the emotional distance I was creating had actually pushed him through and away from the phone.

"I do not want to ever have this discussion with you again. I will not shift how incredibly connected and safe I finally feel when it comes to my relationship with the powers that be, especially when I forged these connections **despite** your destructive influence on my view of God, Jesus, religion, all of it. You are quite literally the biggest hypocrite and deluded individual I have ever had the displeasure of knowing- **fully** knowing. I wish I never knew you- not this way. We'd be better off as strangers." I huffed a bitter laugh. "You've always put on your best act for store clerks and church members, and anyone else who has the opportunity to know you on a surface level. Lucky for them, too, because knowing you any deeper runs the risk of being manipulated to serve each and every one of **your** needs."

His voice quavered, on the edge of breaking. "Annie. Please."

"Don't. You don't get to call me that. You don't get to address me like a beloved friend; like a cherished loved one. You don't fucking know me. You don't fucking know anything about me except for the things you make up about me. You've never accepted me as I am, and you never will. That's why I'm done. With this conversation. With your bullshit. With you."

"Jenna Anne, you can't say things like that! You will

not speak to me that way! You are my **daughter**. YOU **WILL** RESPECT ME."

"I have never respected you. You don't deserve my respect. Go find the admiration that you are so desperate for from all those people you trick into believing you're some pious man of God. Go lean on those that don't know you like I do, and forget about me. Forget everything you think you know about me. Forget the stories. Forget the way I've begged you to see me and love me where I'm at. Forget the years spent pining for your attention. Forget all of it. In fact, Luke..." I took a breath to steady myself as I delivered the killing blow. "Forget my fucking name."

I ended the call, and- without restraint- threw my phone into the still wet paint on the wall across from where I sat trembling with rage. It clattered to the floor leaving a blue rectangle stain on the carpet. No matter how many coats I applied, I could still see the indention my phone left in the drywall- a constant reminder of the storm only he could pull from me. I collapsed into tears and curled into myself, making my body as small as I could in an attempt to shrink into nothingness. The last words I said to him played over and over in my mind as I drifted into a nightmare fueled sleep.

Forget my name.
Forget my name.
Forget my fucking name.

chapter one
be careful what you wish for

"He doesn't remember anything."

The words rang through my body, echoing down corridors long since sealed shut.

"What do you mean 'anything'?" I asked, wide-eyed, brows furrowed, air quotes lingering as my body moved at a sloth's pace.

The air felt thick.

"Ma'am. I mean to say, he has no idea he has any children. He knows his name, what he likes," she paused, tilting her head towards me, "and what he doesn't like. He makes himself *abundantly* clear about those things." I had a feeling I knew what she meant.

"A-and, you know... beyond a shadow of a doubt... he's... he's not faking it? L-lying?"

She could sense the years of trauma and distrust wafting off of me like mist billowing from a churning, angry sea.

"Oh, my dear," she cooed, head slightly cocked, with eyes softened to deliver what would normally be terrible news. "Brain scans don't lie. That is not the man you knew in there."

A sigh made its way from the depths of my being. My body must have been holding it for just such an occasion. "...oh..." I muttered from under eyelashes that hid welling tears. Once again, she seemed to know what I wasn't saying as I silently washed back and forth in the tumultuous tides of my emotions.

He doesn't remember me.
Why does that make me feel... glad?
*Why does **that** make me feel guilty?*
Why do I feel... angry?
How could he forget me...
How could he forget me?

I felt wounded beyond my capacity to heal.

I had been forgotten.

Erased.

Eradicated from his life as if I had never existed at all.

Maybe secretly how he had always wanted.

I was furious at the betrayal.

I had given him so much of my life. My energy. My tears. Only to be swept away like a dream fading from view the moment it is recalled.

Logically, I knew science wasn't personal. Disease wasn't personal. The thing about heart-centered events, though, is they don't tend to lean into our rationale.

No.

Grief loves to wax poetic. It is, perhaps, the most obnoxious experience we have as humans. It plunges us into deep, unyielding despair, only to lift us spewing and sputtering to the surface, revealing truths we couldn't have discovered without it.

Absolutely disgusting behavior, honestly.

I didn't realize I had drifted away until I felt a hand gently lift my own, and place a tissue into my palm. She was looking at me with those same soft, knowing eyes.

"Would you like me to tell you about the man we have been caring for?" quickly adding- surely for my own benefit, "The one he seems to think he is?"

What a strange thing to hear at 11:30 on a Tuesday morning.

Would you like me to tell you all about someone you've known your entire life?

I knew that was not the way she had intended it to be received, but the petulant child running my limbic system would not be swayed to believe otherwise. She queued up a knee-jerk reaction unbecoming of the woman I had grown into, so I clamped down on her preferred response, and instead nodded wordlessly- a needed precaution for what might have escaped my normally grounded and centered being.

"Well, he loves singing, and playing the guitar. His brother tells us he has always loved music, and performing. He performs for our staff and residents all the time."

Part of me, the aforementioned broken-hearted child, wanted to say he had been performing for everyone but the ones who counted for years. That I would have preferred to have only known his stage persona. I quieted my inner child with a knowing squeeze of her little hand.

I know, little girl. I know. I see you.

The corner of my lips tipped up in a solemn smile, "Yea, he has always loved the spotlight. How is his playing? Now that..." I trailed off, suddenly realizing there were a few pieces of him I would've kept alive.

Awake.

"Oh he's wonderful! Most of our residents with advanced cases still retain their ability to play instruments, write poetry, sing, paint. It is lovely to know- when everything else is gone- our connection to creativity remains."

Twin tears escaped my eyes, each shed for a different reason. They raced down my cheeks, leaving trails in my makeup to mark their passing. The compassionate part of my heart was struck by the sentimentality of it all, while my raging heartache demanded justice for being left behind; tasked with remembering what his brain mercifully allowed him to forget. "That is lovely," I said more resolute than I meant to, the cynic in me still leading the charge. The woman's eyes were soft again. It seemed like she might perpetually be in a state of kindness, compassion, and... was that... pity? I had to look away to avoid rage weeping.

...please don't look at me that way. Please don't ever look at me that way. I don't need your pity. I need you to tell me you can see where I'm coming from. I need you to tell me I'm right to feel this way. That you see through his dementia riddled personality, down to the monstrous version of him I know too well. Maybe more than anyone.

I straightened- I had apparently been steadily slumping under the weight of a lifetime of paternal disappointment, and the heavy juxtaposition of my warring emotions. "S-so..." I internally kicked myself for stammering so much, for my voice giving me away. I set to fiddling with a pendant that hung low around my neck to redirect the nervous energy in my body toward something innocuous while I attempted to settle myself. A small voice tried to reassure me that I could be vulnerable, all while my ego donned the mask I wore when I felt less than steady. "He sounds like he's doing well here," I offered, finally. She smiled and reached to gently squeeze my arm just above my elbow. "If it helps," she spoke quietly now, "his faults are not hidden. He shows us what I can only assume is a fraction of the wounded man you were subjected to. I am under no guise that he has ever been so consistently pleasant before."

I caught her phrasing. "Subjected to" and "wounded" hung in the air like smoke off of an incense burner. Cleansing and simultaneously a bit suffocating. I felt seen. I suppose- now more than ever- his tendency to hide behind bravado and indignation would be limited, only coming about in moments of lucidity. Strange, how dementia seemed to strip him of his masks, forcing him to show up as the version of himself he had buried long before I was, as she said, "subjected" to the worst parts of him. It seemed, in an attempt to escape the monsters he fled from, he chose to embody them as a way to hide amongst them. Only, instead of escaping unscathed, after years of blending in with his demons, he had become one of them. The little boy inside of him who needed love and healing was tossed to the wolves to quiet his pleas, effectively erasing the part of him he longed to protect. Until now.

"Wounded? H-how do you know he's... wounded?" I rather disliked the feeling of that word in my mouth in relation to someone who had hurt others as he was hurt- someone who chose to carry on generations of pain, only to pass it along to everyone he encountered that was meant to matter. Once again, the evolved, more understanding part of my heart stepped forward to remind me multiple things could be true at once. He could be both the victim of abuse, and the abuser. Both hurting, and the cause of pain. Wasn't I the same? Hadn't I been hurt, and in my unhealed states passed that hurt onto others? Hadn't I left a trail of broken hearts in my wake before I stopped making my pain everyone else's problem? Passing the responsibility to heal onto unwitting participants in my journey to becoming a kinder, more self-aware being? I wasn't even *alone* in that journey. I knew countless others who had learned the hard way how it feels to reckon with the wounds they inflicted on others before they grew into the versions of themselves I knew and loved. Why then, was it so hard to allow him to exist as a complex human, same as me?

"He..." she started, hesitating for what seemed like an eternity before she finally added, "There was an altercation. One we know was born out of confusion. He seemed to think he was interacting with his father, and became quite agitated, to say the least."

"Agitated? How Agitated? Did he hurt someone?"
My stomach was in knots.

"No, no, dear. Nothing of lasting effect. Nothing our staff hasn't witnessed before. We are quite accustomed to residents occasionally lashing out from confusion."

Lashing out. She said the words so nonchalantly I almost didn't feel them slice into my side. Memories came flooding in of uncontrollable fits of anger, drunken nights spent picking fights or- worse yet- recklessly driving all over town. I remembered one awful night best left forgotten. Unlike my father, though, I had no such luck of erasing this memory. I was just thirteen. It was the night before a family trip to a local amusement park. Dinner went awry when he had disappeared after an argument he had manifested out of thin air, like a

80

magic trick no one had asked for. He returned home hours later, in the middle of the night, three sheets to the wind and shouting loud enough for the neighbors to hear. "You don't love me! You all hate me! I'm going to kill myself! I'm going to do it, because of *you*!" he bellowed, pointing at my step mother in the driveway. I shamefully remembered being embarrassed, and silently wondering if we'd still get to go to Six Flags in the morning. I remembered hoping God couldn't hear me when I thought, "If he's going to kill himself, I wish he would just keep quiet about it. I have been looking forward to this trip for weeks." It wasn't the first time I had been so severely critical of him and his existence in my life. This followed the death of my grandpa, who- to this day- was the only man who felt like a father to me. I had renounced any and all gods who would condone taking my grandfather, and leaving me with *him*.

Another memory crept in on the tail of the last, reminding me of the moment I pulled my step mom aside and pleaded with her to take my sisters, to run back to where she came from. I was narrowly nine years old. With tears in my eyes, I begged her, "Please. Don't stay here. Pack all of your things, grab my sisters, and go to your mama's. She won't let him get to you." I had full faith the whirlwind that was my step-granny was one of the few people my father was intimidated by. She wasn't one to tolerate bullshit, and according to her, "He's damn near chock full of it." I couldn't bring myself to disagree with her.

"Ma'am?"

"Jenna. Call me Jenna."

Softening over and over, she said, "Jenna. It is up to you as to whether or not you want to see him. You get to decide, and no amount of judgement comes with whatever decision you make. There is no shame in staying; there is no shame in leaving. I get the feeling there's a part of him, a piece of him buried so deep he couldn't access it, that would want you to do what's best for *you*. Past the damaged, unhealed parts of his heart, there is a father who loves his daughter to the capacity he could love anything- of that I'm sure. The choice lies with you and you alone. I'll give you some space to decide."

She squeezed my arm once more, and walked into her office, leaving me standing between the exit and the doors to the common area where my father sat unaware of my existence. I stood motionless, attempting to feel any nod this way or that from my insides. My instincts must have been numbed by the lingering shock, because they sat quietly anticipating my decision with no guidance one way or the other. I willed my feet to move, left or right- I didn't care.

Just make a decision. Leave what could be for the next decision. Left? Or right?

I turned left, moved to the exit that led away from the numerous triggers the common area would provide, and walked out into drizzling rain. The weather seemed to empathize with my confused and broken heart. I walked slowly to catch every drop on my cheeks, letting the rain blend with the tears that poured from my eyes. I turned my gaze skyward to ask the powers that be, "Will I ever walk away from him unscathed?" The clouds split open, turning a spring shower into a torrential downpour. A flash of lightning and a crack of thunder seemed to say what I already knew: interacting with him in any capacity would always be akin to weathering a storm, and if I wasn't prepared I could be swept away, never to be found again.

82

Acknowledgements

Releasing *Being Human* in 2022 was a gift to my inner child who dreamt of telling stories (specifically my own) and writing books. Since then, my little self has tagged along on adventures big and small. From publishing a second book, speaking my truth and upholding boundaries, and making new friends, the child version of me has held my hand and cheered me on the whole way.

Inviting her into my spaces by surrounding myself with her favorite things, and showing up for Me the way she never knew how has mended my relationship with my Self in ways I could have never anticipated. The magic and wonder that trails her as she skips about my energy enlivens my day, and keeps me going when I feel like giving up.

This second edition is a love letter to all the versions of myself that keep my head above water when the sea is raging, and who celebrate the sunshine with me, and build castles on the beach. This one is for you. They're all for you.

Jb, you already know what you mean to my life. Our journey together has been filled with so many twists and turns, there was no way to know where we would end up. You're the backroad to my midnight drive, and I couldn't imagine my life without you in it. Thank you for evolving with me, and for never failing to dodge and weave when our journey went off-roading. Our lives may not have led where we expected, but I am more and more grateful by the day for the way we prioritized *us*. We never failed to put our friendship first. Letting our dynamic reveal itself to us has been one of the scariest but most rewarding experiences I've ever explored before. I know we can make it through anything as long as we have each other (and you're stuck with me, buckaroo). Here's to a lifetime of laughter, silly inside jokes, and cheering each other on wherever our lives lead us.

Cassidy. Family Hands, Family Hearts. Public Relations Extraordinaire. You are a gift to my life I never knew I needed. One I could never go without, now. It's selfish, I'm sure, but I'm going to need you to love me forever, kthanks. I am so excited for the adventures we will continue to have together. I know, no matter where my journey takes me, I have a cherished confidante for life. It is one of my greatest honors to be not only cousins, but friends. Witnessing you continues to be so inspiring. You remind me what bravery looks like, so I can emulate you in my shakier moments. Thank you for being here. I love you forever.

Jaime & Hass (Cass you're here, too!), we make up the smallest- and most formidable- girl gang. From the unbridled support and love, to showing up to my events and showing out no matter how "small" the venue, you sure know how to make a girl feel like a bonafide author. You'd think **publishing books** would do the trick, but it wasn't until you each helped me get ready for a reading at an ice cream shop as if you were preparing me for a red carpet event that I felt... real. Much like in *The Velveteen Rabbit* your care and compassion brought me to life in ways I could not have seen coming. Thank you endlessly, Jaime, for sending love letters in the form of music and playlists, and witnessing me in my darker moments, but never baulking. Hassica, thank you for your expert Bitch Wrangling™ and for every way you see me and express so beautifully my experience from your point of view. You have such a knack for reminding me where I've been, and how far I've come. Cassidy. What else can I say? Way more, for sure, but what I will add is that I know I can count on you. That is rare in my life, so to be able to count on you to be there for me is a gift I will forever strive to match. You literally gave me the bra off your back for my reading, just because mine felt bad to my neurospicy brain. Who does that? You do, that's who. Could not have a better friend, Sam Wrangler, or PRE.

Detrimentumxx, I will likely never call you by your name (in fact I often have to remind myself that "Det" is not your government name), but I *will* forever call you my friend. I cannot wait to hold your creations in my hands, carrying them everywhere I go, showing them off to anyone who even looks like they love a happily ever after. "My friend, Det, wrote this book. Sure, yea, Jessica Norton, that's her name, but Det is her name name. Anyway, you like books? I got a great one for ya." It's sure to spark interest, I know it. I am so grateful to be on this publishing journey alongside each other. Just two write-or-dies taking on the world of words and stories woven for the masses. You better get some great sunglasses, because our future is lookin' bright. Are you teary-eyed? I bet you're teary-eyed. Teehee.

To my personal STAY cheer squad: Your support of my creations and my journey without ever having met me in person just proves a bunch of kpop friend tropes, and I'm so here for it. Thank you, endlessly, for every way you've shown up in my life. You make this Stray Kid Stay.

To the staff and pals I've made at CCC: I couldn't have finished this book just *anywhere*. The way you all cheer me on and create such a welcoming space for little weirdos like me is a kindness I didn't realize I was missing in most of my writing spots. Thank you for all the support, for Beta Reading, for welcoming me to read new pieces out loud to practice speaking in front of others, for regularly telling me how much you all enjoy my company... I have found friends where I didn't expect them to be, and I am so beyond grateful for your presence in my life. Here's to the coolest book launch anyone has ever had (and the coolest friends to celebrate with).

To my family and friends, you all enrich my life in your own ways, and I am forever grateful to each one of you for showing up the way you do. Thank you for evolving alongside me, for showing up for yourselves the way you show up for others, for your love, and support. I yam what I yam, because you love me (and helped teach me how to love me, too).

Once again, and as always, to those of you who helped shape who I am by giving me the opportunity to stand up for myself, to show up in a way that was scary but brave, thank you. I know life will serve up more opportunities to show myself who I've become; who I'm becoming. I am grateful to you for helping me learn what it feels like to let go, to love myself first, to trust the process. The challenges only get bigger from here, so thank you for helping me see that I can trust myself, be satisfied with my love for me, and to only accept what is for me, what serves my life with love. I hope you're out there learning and growing and accepting only what serves your highest and greatest good. I hope you are learning to love you. I hope you are learning how to trust yourself to take care of you. I hope you are experiencing growth beyond measure with all the support and ample love to see you through the arduous task that is going inward. I am sending you all the best vibes. Here's to you, and me, and all of us as we traverse each of our journeys Being Human. After all...

We signed up for this

Being Human

you signed up for this

Sam Razberry

Made in the USA
Monee, IL
14 October 2024

67895593R00059